DESPERADOES
AND
DYNAMITE

DESPERADOES

AND

DYNAMITE

TRAIN ROBBERY IN THE UNITED STATES

BY DIANE YANCEY

Franklin Watts
New York London Toronto Sydney
A First Book 1991

To Michael, my best friend.

Cover photograph copyright © Historical Pictures Service, Chicago

Photographs copyright ©: Scala/Art Resource Inc., N.Y.: pp. 8, 13; The Bettmann Archive: pp. 16, 24, 37; Historical Pictures Service, Chicago: pp. 18, 20, 35, 42; Culver Pictures, Inc.: pp. 22, 31, 41; Wyoming State Museum: pp. 25, 27, 39, 49, 52; New York Public Library, Picture Collection: p. 45.

Library of Congress Cataloging-in-Publication Data
Yancey, Diane.
Desperadoes and dynamite / by Diane Yancey.
p.   cm.—(A First book)
Includes bibliographical references and index.
Summary: Describes some famous train robberies of the Old West and the involvement of such notorious outlaws as Jesse James, Butch Cassidy and the Sundance Kid, and the Dalton Gang.
ISBN 0-531-20038-8
1. Outlaws—West (U.S.)—History—Juvenile literature.   2. Train robberies—West (U.S.)—History—Juvenile literature.   3. West (U.S).—History—1848–1950—Juvenile literature. [1. Robbers and outlaws. 2. West (U.S)—History—1848–1950.] I. Title.
II. Series.
F596.Y36   1991
364.1′552′0978—dc20   91-12149 CIP   AC

CONTENTS

INTRODUCTION

On a cold, wet Saturday night in 1866, the Ohio and Mississippi passenger train was making good time on its run from St. Louis, Missouri, to Cincinnati, Ohio.

Behind the locomotive and the tender (the car carrying coal and water for the steam engine) followed the express car. Money and important papers sent by rail were locked in safes in this car. These special cars were owned by express companies, not the railroad. They had no windows and carried no passengers; the sliding door on the side was supposed to be locked at all times.

The express car on the Ohio and Mississippi was owned by the Adams Express Company, and messenger Elem Miller was guarding the safes inside.

But messenger Miller, like many other guards, was

The express car, third car back, had
its own guard and was supposed to be the
most secure part of the train.

not always careful. On the night of October 6, 1866, when the train pulled out of the little town of Seymour, Indiana, Miller had not locked the sliding door.

As the train left Seymour, two men wearing masks swung onto the small front platform of the express car. Unseen, they sneaked down the running board and entered the car.

The men drew revolvers and ordered Miller to open the safe but Miller only had the key to the "local" safe, the one he opened along the line. The safe containing more valuable items, the "through" safe, could only be opened by officials in Cincinnati.

While Miller opened the local safe, the robbers pulled the brake cord, which signaled the train to stop.

The express companies fitted the heavy safes with rollers on the bottom and a ring at each end for easy loading and unloading at the end of the line. Thus it was no problem for the masked men to roll the "through" safe to the door and push it out.

One of the holdup men pulled the brake cord again, the signal for the train to go ahead. As it picked up speed, the bandits stepped off and disappeared into the night. They were quickly left far behind with about $15,000 in loot.

Alone with one empty safe, messenger Miller sat staring into the dark night. He had no way of knowing that he was part of one of the first train robberies in United States history. He was just horrified that the theft had been so easy!

CHAPTER ONE
THE EARLY YEARS

Soldiers who had lived through the battles of the Civil War returned to their homes in 1866. They quickly discovered that their land was in ruins, they had no money, and there were no jobs. These men were used to danger and excitement; some of them were not afraid to break the law.

Robbing a bank was a quick way to get money, but it was also risky. Lawmen and eager townspeople made getaways dangerous.

Holding up stagecoaches had paid off in the past. Bandits like Rattlesnake Dick, Tom Bell, and Black Bart became notorious for robbing the strongboxes carried by stagecoaches. But now express companies were sending gold and valuables by rail because stagecoaches had been attacked so often.

Between 1830 and 1850, railroads had expanded until over 30,000 miles (48,000 km) of track covered the United States. When the transcontinental railroad was finished in 1869, the Central Pacific and Union Pacific railroads linked the East with the West. Passengers and goods could now cross the entire United States by railroad.

The trains ran through lonely stretches of country, making stops at small, out-of-the-way stations. The express cars were lightly guarded. Consequently, many dishonest men decided to try train robbery as a way to make their living.

One day after the Seymour train robbery (pulled off by the Reno brothers, a band of neighborhood thugs), robbers near Bristow, Kentucky, pulled a rail loose on the Louisville and Nashville line. The locomotive ran off the tracks and turned over. In the confusion that followed, the train wreckers smashed in the express car door and got away with $8,000.

A third robbery took place on November 9, 1866, near Franklin, Kentucky. A passenger train was robbed after it hit a barrier of crossties and jumped the track.

The next September, again near Seymour, Indiana, two farm boys robbed an eastbound Ohio and Mississippi passenger train of $8,000.

At first, train robberies occurred only east of the Mississippi River. But trains in the lawless western frontier were too tempting for robbers to ignore for long.

In 1848, John Marshall discovered gold near Coloma, California. Wells-Fargo, the company that owned most of the banking and express business in California, sent gold to New York City banks by stagecoach. But by 1869, the express company began sending their gold east by railroad. The company believed that using the faster trains would do away with the problem of holdups.

Wells-Fargo was mistaken.

The first train robbery in the West took place on November 4, 1870. The "Seven Knights of the Road," including their leader "Gentleman Jack" Davis, gathered near the train station at Verdi, Nevada, in the Sierra Nevada Mountains. They wanted to go over the final details of their plan.

Gentleman Jack's neighbors didn't know he was an outlaw. To them, Jack was a gentle, shy rancher who raised flowers as a hobby. He was an accepted member of society; he was also a careful leader of his robber band.

On the night of November 4, Central Pacific Train Number 1 slowed for the Verdi station. Three of the robbers slipped unseen onto the train. They stopped it a short distance out of Verdi and overpowered the Wells-Fargo guard. Then they emptied the strong box and escaped without one shot being fired.

Stagecoaches were held up quite easily, so banks began to use the railroad. Who would have thought that soon trains would also be robbed?

Wells-Fargo offered a $10,000 reward and put their best detective, F. T. Burke, on the case. Burke was a resourceful and determined agent with a reputation for "getting his man." With a handpicked posse, he tracked the bandits over the Sierra Nevadas. Within four days of the robbery, the "Seven Knights of the Road" were safely locked in jail.

Over $39,000 of the stolen gold coins was recovered. The remaining $3,000 was never found. According to some, the money remains hidden in the Sierra Nevadas, waiting to be discovered.

CHAPTER TWO
THE OUTLAW'S TRAIL

In legend, Jesse James was the first person to pull off a train robbery in the United States. Actually, by the time James looted his first express car, train robbery was a seven-year-old problem.

James became an outlaw in 1866, when he was only eighteen. He and his brother Frank held up a bank and murdered a man in Liberty, Missouri. Killing meant little to Jesse. He was a Civil War veteran, already responsible for over 100 deaths during the war, one of them that of a minister.

Countless robberies and murders later, on July 21, 1873, the James brothers and their gang pulled a rail from under the eastbound express train on the Chicago, Rock Island, and Pacific line near Adair, Iowa. The locomotive turned over, and steam from the boiler

This old photo was discovered in a saloon in New Mexico. Supposedly, Jesse James is at right, Frank James is at left, and their mother is in the middle.

scalded the engineer to death. The gang escaped with an unknown amount of cash.

Wrecking was a popular way of stopping trains in the early days of train robbery. A train could be wrecked in three ways: a half-open switch, a barricade on the track, or a loosened rail.

Switches—sections of track used to guide trains from one railroad track to another—were often located near towns or stations. Wreckers usually kept away from them. They preferred to pull a rail from ahead of a train at the last minute or to lay a barricade of logs across the tracks. Wreckers were the most hated of outlaws because of their disregard for innocent lives.

Since bank robbery was Jesse James's specialty, it was almost a year before he robbed another train. When he did, he and his men simply held up a train stopped at a depot. They got away with $7,000. Before he rode off, Jesse shouted to the conductor, "When you see the reporters, tell 'em you were talking to Jesse James!"

Large rewards were posted for the capture of the outlaw and his gang. But the wily bandit was hard to catch.

In 1875, the James gang robbed a train near Muncie, Indiana. After a brush with death while holding up the bank in Northfield, Minnesota, the

$5,000 REWARD

JESSE JAMES

For Train Robbery

Notify AUTHORITIES
LIBERTY, MISSOURI

Rewards would go even higher than
the $5,000 offered here for the capture
of Jesse James and his gang.

brothers went back to Missouri. There they struck the Chicago and Alton Railroad on October 7, 1879.

In 1881 the James gang shot and killed a conductor and a passenger while robbing a train near Winston, Missouri. Governor T. T. Crittenden heard about the vicious attack and offered the enormous sum of $10,000 for the capture of the outlaws.

To get the reward, a new member of the James gang, Robert Ford, turned traitor. During a meeting to plan a bank robbery, Ford shot James in the back of the head. Jesse James died on April 3, 1882. He was thirty-four years old.

The Men and Their Methods

James's death was big news, but even before his death, newspapers across the country had written about train robberies in great detail.

The papers reported that trains were held up on deserted sections of track or near tiny stations. Readers knew that it was standard practice for gangs to be made up of at least six outlaws: two would cover the crew with their guns, two would guard the passengers, and two would break into the express car. Words like "blind baggage" and "torpedo signal" were familiar to everyone.

The "blind baggage"—the platform at the front of the windowless express car—was in just the right place

Jesse James, was killed by a member of his own gang, who shot James from behind.

for outlaws to board a train. The coal-filled tender car hid the robbers from the locomotive crew. In this position, the robbers were in a perfect place to take over the train and rob the express car.

In the early days, train robbers also used "torpedo signals" to stop a train. Torpedo signals were tiny, harmless explosives placed on the track that made a sharp noise when a locomotive ran over them. Railroads used them to warn engineers of danger ahead on the tracks. A good engineer always stopped the train when a torpedo signal went off.

Young Sam Bass put a red lantern on the tracks to stop his first train in Texas in 1877. A red lantern was a common signal for trouble ahead. Sam got away with over $60,000. During a later robbery, however, he ran into trouble: the messenger refused to unlock the express car door.

Messengers had become more careful about locking their cars after the news of the first robberies. Robbers were forced to knock down the locked doors, which often took a long time. And once inside, the outlaws still had to deal with an armed messenger waiting for them.

Bass, imaginative and ruthless, threatened to burn the express car if the messenger did not unlock the door. This threat became a common one for the next twenty years.

Outlaw Rube Burrows came up with a new twist

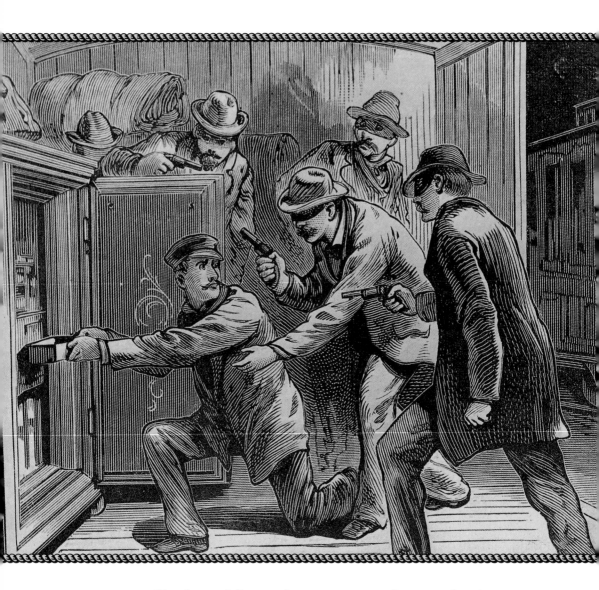

**Train robbers force a guard to unlock
a safe and hand over its contents.**

to get into an express car. Burrows was an honest farmboy from Alabama before he held up his first train in late 1866. He was the first outlaw to threaten to shoot the train crew if the express messenger did not open the door. His threat was also used for many years, although few train robbers actually carried it out.

The real solution to the problem of opening an express car was dynamite. Before 1890, robbers tried black powder and nitroglycerin, but both could blow up unexpectedly. Dynamite was more stable, making it just the thing for blasting through the door and opening the safe.

California train robbers Chris Evans and John Sontag used dynamite during their attacks against the Southern Pacific Railroad from 1890 until 1893. Hot-tempered Sontag had a grudge against Southern Pacific. He had been crippled while working for them as a brakeman. Evans was sympathetic and did not mind a little dishonest work. Carrying shotguns, the two men looted express cars until August 1893, when they were captured in the Sierra Nevada Mountains of California.

Although dynamite was popular, many outlaws never learned to handle it correctly. A famous example was Butch Cassidy's attack on the Overland Flyer in 1892.

During this attack, the gang blew out the side of the express car and knocked the messenger uncon-

The infamous
Rube Burrows was
displayed in his
casket when
he died.

On June 2, 1899, this train was
blown up by dynamite. This is
the view from inside the mail car.

scious. Then, still using too big of a charge, they exploded the safe, scattering money in all directions.

The Long Riders

While opening the express car was a challenge to train robbers, the biggest problem they faced was getting away with the money. The most glamorous and dramatic of the escape artists were the "long riders."

Long riders got their name because they held up a train or a bank and then rode for hours or days to escape the posse that trailed them. They specialized in bank and train robbery, but the excitement of living one step ahead of death was just as important to them as the money they stole.

Butch Cassidy, born with the name George Leroy Parker, was the most famous and charming of the long riders. He pulled off his first train robbery on November 3, 1887, when he was twenty years old. In 1896, after several years of drifting and petty crimes, he became the leader of the largest gang in the West—the "Wild Bunch."

The Wild Bunch included a variety of long riders: gentlemanly Harry Longabaugh (the Sundance Kid); Harvey Logan (Kid Curry), the meanest member of the gang; soft-spoken Elzy Lay, Butch's best friend; George "Flat Nose" Curry, who reportedly turned to crime for the fun of it; Ben Kilpatrick (the "Tall Texan"); and his steady girlfriend, Laura Bullion.

Butch Cassidy is one of the most famous outlaws in U.S. history.

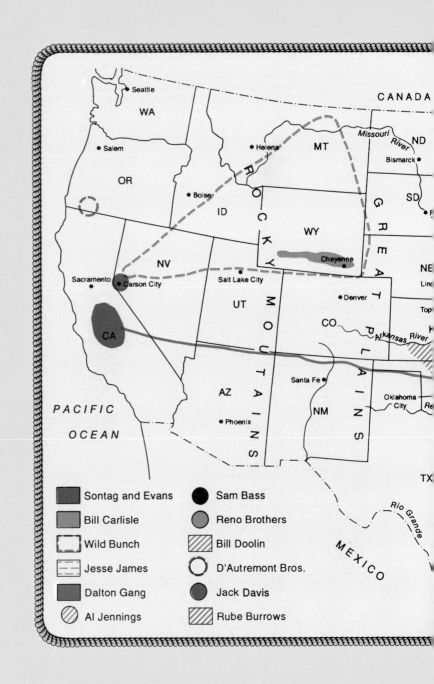

Sontag and Evans
Bill Carlisle
Wild Bunch
Jesse James
Dalton Gang
Al Jennings

Sam Bass
Reno Brothers
Bill Doolin
D'Autremont Bros.
Jack Davis
Rube Burrows

The gang robbed trains in the Rocky Mountain States beginning in June 1889. Part of their success lay in Butch's carefully planned getaways. Before a robbery, he planted teams of fresh horses, chosen for speed and strength, across the country. Sometimes, three relay teams were used to cover long distances.

The Wild Bunch broke up after their last successful holdup on July 3, 1901, during which they stole $40,000.

With money to travel, Butch Cassidy and the Sundance Kid headed to South America. They began robbing banks and trains there in 1905. According to reports, they were killed in 1909 in San Vicente, Bolivia. Some people say, however, that Cassidy survived the shoot-out. They say he returned to the Pacific Northwest and lived there until 1937.

While Cassidy was forming the Wild Bunch in Wyoming, the Daltons were robbing trains in California and Oklahoma. Despite their short career as outlaws, no long rider gang had a more infamous record of robbery and murder than the Daltons.

The Dalton brothers—Robert (Bob), Emmett, Grattan, and William (Bill)—began their careers as law officers in Kansas. However, Bob and Grattan soon lost their badges for stealing horses. Bob had already killed a man in a fight over a woman. Shortly after that, the brothers formed a gang and began stealing in earnest. In 1891 they robbed their first train in California.

Some members of the Wild Bunch: seated from left to right are Harry Longabaugh, Ben Kilpatrick, and Butch Cassidy; standing from left to right are Bill Carver and Harvey Logan.

They escaped back to the Midwest with the law on their trail and continued holding up trains and banks. In July 1892, they robbed the Missouri, Kansas and Texas Express in the little town of Adair, Oklahoma. A battle with a group of railroad detectives ended with the Daltons killing all of them. One innocent bystander was wounded, and another died.

The brothers went on robbing until October 5, 1892. On that day, Bob and Grattan were killed in a bank robbery shoot-out in their home town of Coffeyville, Kansas. Emmett survived and was captured. He was sentenced to life imprisonment in the Kansas State Penitentiary. Bill Dalton continued to rob banks and trains and was killed during a holdup in September 1895.

CHAPTER THREE

A CALL FOR HEROES

Train robbers were always nervous about trouble coming from the passengers or train crew. They didn't need to be worried, however. Despite a reputation for reckless courage, westerners were afraid to face a gang of armed bandits. Lawyer-turned-outlaw Al Jennings claimed that a robber just had to "smash the glass" (break a window) with a bullet to keep curious passengers from sticking their heads out of the train.

Newspapers in the 1870s reported that few people—passengers, railroad police, or express messengers—ever tried to stop a train robbery during the actual event.

Average travelers were too busy hiding their gold watches and pocket money under their seats to be heroes. If trouble came, it was usually from a peace officer who happened to be on board. Even this was uncommon as an officer was almost helpless when outnumbered by a gang of robbers.

The duties of the early railroad police included catching pickpockets and controlling freight and ticket thefts. When train robbery became a problem, railroad companies quickly added more police to their force. But these newly hired police often received no instructions. They had no knowledge of the law. They were handed a badge, a revolver, and a club and then sent out to work. These untrained police had trouble defending a train against armed outlaws.

Not even the law helped the railroad police. It stated that railroad police could arrest train robbers only while the robbers were on railroad property. As soon as the robbers stepped off the property, the railroad police could not follow; the local police had to pick up the trail. By the time the robbery was reported to a nearby town, the outlaws were far away.

Because express companies had the most to lose, they led the fight against train robbery.

After their first express car was robbed in 1866, Adams Express Company called in the Pinkerton National Detective Agency.

Allan Pinkerton, who had been a barrel-maker in Scotland, founded the Pinkerton Agency in 1850 in

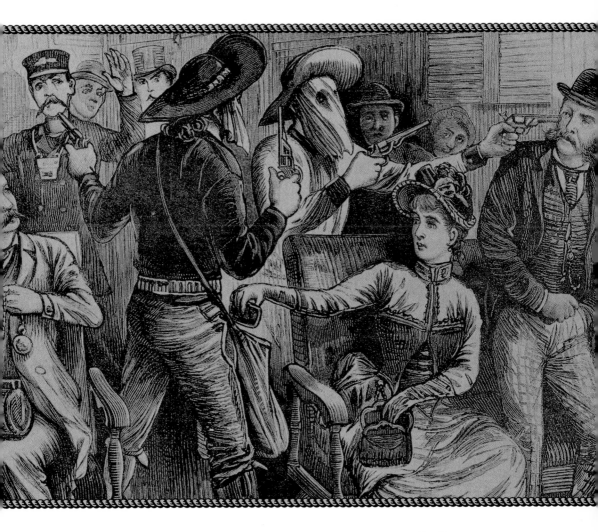

When robbers waving pistols boarded
a train, there wasn't much passengers
could do, except give up their valuables.

Chicago, Illinois. It was the first private detective agency in the city and one of the first in the country.

Pinkerton and his two sons, Robert and William, tackled every case with amazing thoroughness and determination. When the Pinkertons set out to catch a criminal, they did not stop until they either jailed the criminal or had proof the outlaw was dead. One Pinkerton detective demanded that a buried train robber be dug up and photographed before he closed his case.

The Pinkertons caught outlaws by sending detectives, called operatives, to the neighborhood of the crime. Often the operatives put on disguises and went undercover. They pretended to be traveling salesmen or tramps and chatted with possible witnesses.

After the first robbery in Seymour, operative Dick Winscott played the part of a bartender in John Reno's favorite saloon. He had photos of John Reno taken for Allan Pinkerton's files.

One of Pinkerton's most talented operatives, Charles Siringo, was sometimes called "an almost unshakable bloodhound." Siringo posed as an outlaw and joined Butch Cassidy's gang for several years. His identity was later discovered by the gang, and he had to run for his life.

Pinkerton operatives were skillful, but not all of them were admirable men. Tom Horn had a special talent for tracking down train robbers. He was noto-

Pinkerton's National Detective Agency.

FOUNDED BY ALLAN PINKERTON, 1850.

Principals. {ROBT. A. PINKERTON, New York, / WM. A. PINKERTON, Chicago.}

GEO. D. BANGS, General Manager, New York.
ALLAN PINKERTON, Assistant General Manager, New York.

JOHN CORNISH, Gen'l Sup't., Eastern Division, New York.
EDWARD S. GAYLOR, Gen'l Sup't., Middle Division, Chicago.
JAMES McPARLAND, Gen'l Sup't., Western Division, Denver.

Attorneys: GUTHRIE, CRAVATH & HENDERSON, New York.

TELEPHONE CONNECTION.

REPRESENTING THE AMERICAN BANKERS' ASSOCIATION.

OFFICES.

DENVER, OPERA HOUSE BLOCK, J. C. FRASER, Sup't.
NEW YORK, 57 BROADWAY
BOSTON, 30 COURT STREET
PHILADELPHIA, 441 CHESTNUT AVENUE
MONTREAL, MERCHANTS BANK BUILDING
CHICAGO, 201 FIFTH AVENUE
ST. PAUL, GERMANIA BANK BUILDING
ST. LOUIS, WAINWRIGHT BUILDING
KANSAS CITY, 422 MAIN STREET
PORTLAND, ORE. MARQUAM BLOCK
SEATTLE, WASH. BAILEY BLOCK
SAN FRANCISCO, CROCKER BUILDING

$4,000.00 REWARD.

CIRCULAR No. 2.

DENVER, Colo., January 24th, 1902.

THE FIRST NATIONAL BANK OF WINNEMUCCA, Nevada, a member of THE AMERICAN BANKERS' ASSOCIATION, was robbed of $32,640 at the noon hour, September 19th, 1900, by three men who entered the bank and "held up" the cashier and four other persons. Two of the robbers carried revolvers and a third a Winchester rifle. They compelled the five persons to go into the inner office of the bank while the robbery was committed.

At least $31,000 was in $20 gold coin ; $1,200 in $5 and $10 gold coin ; the balance in currency, including one $5 bill.

Since the issuance of our first circular, dated Denver, Colo., May 15th, 1901, it has been positively determined that two of the men who committed this robbery were :

1. **GEORGE PARKER,** alias "BUTCH" CASSIDY, alias GEORGE CASSIDY, alias INGERFIELD.
2. **HARRY LONGBAUGH,** alias "KID" LONGBAUGH, alias HARRY ALONZO, alias "THE SUNDANCE KID,"

PARKER and LONGBAUGH are members of the HARVEY LOGAN alias "KID" CURRY band of bank and train (express) "hold up" robbers.

For the arrest, detention and surrender to an authorized officer of the State of Nevada of each or any one of the men who robbed the FIRST NATIONAL BANK OF WINNEMUCCA, the following rewards are offered :

BY THE FIRST NATIONAL BANK OF WINNEMUCCA: $1,000 for each robber.
Also 25 per cent., in proportionate shares, on all money recovered.

BY THE AMERICAN BANKERS' ASSOCIATION : $1,000 for each robber.
This reward to be paid on proper identification of either PARKER or LONGBAUGH.

Persons furnishing information leading to the arrest of either or all of the robbers will be entitled to share in the reward.

The outlaws, whose photographs, descriptions and histories appear on this circular MAY ATTEMPT TO CIRCULATE or be in possession of the following described NEW INCOMPLETE BANK NOTES of the NATIONAL BANK OF MONTANA and THE AMERICAN NATIONAL BANK, both of HELENA, MONT., which were stolen by members of the HARVEY LOGAN, alias "KID" CURRY BAND, from the GREAT NORTHERN RAILWAY EXPRESS No. 3, near Wagner, Mont., July 3rd, 1901, by "hold up" methods.

$40,000. INCOMPLETE NEW BANK NOTES of the NATIONAL BANK OF MONTANA (Helena, Montana), $24,000 of which was in ten dollar bills and $16,000 of which was in twenty dollar bills.

> Serial Number 1201 to 2000 inclusive;
> Government Number-Y 934349 to 935148 inclusive;
> Charter Number 5671.

$500. INCOMPLETE BANK NOTES of AMERICAN NATIONAL BANK (Helena, Montana), $300 of which was in ten dollar bills and $200 of which was in twenty dollar bills.

> Serial Number 3423 to 3432 inclusive;
> Government Number V-662761 to V-662770 inclusive;
> Charter Number 4396.

THESE INCOMPLETE BANK NOTES LACKED THE SIGNATURES OF THE PRESIDENTS AND CASHIERS OF THE BANKS NAMED, AND MAY BE CIRCULATED WITHOUT SIGNATURES OR WITH FORGED SIGNATURES.

Chiefs of Police, Sheriffs, Marshals and Constables receiving copy of this circular should furnish a copy of the above described stolen currency to banks, bankers, money brokers, gambling houses, pool room keepers and keepers of disorderly houses, and request their co-operation in the arrest of any person or persons presenting any of these bills.

THE UNITED STATES TREASURY DEPARTMENT REFUSES TO REDEEM THESE STOLEN UNSIGNED OR IMPROPERLY SIGNED NOTES.

Officers are warned to have sufficient assistance and be fully armed, when attempting to arrest either of these outlaws, as they are always heavily armed, and will make a determined resistance before submitting to arrest, not hesitating to kill, if necessary.

Below appear the photographs, descriptions and histories of GEORGE PARKER, alias "BUTCH" CASSIDY, alias GEORGE CASSIDY, alias INGERFIELD and HARRY LONGBAUGH alias HARRY ALONZO.

GEORGE PARKER.
First photograph taken July 15, 1894.

GEORGE PARKER.
Last photograph taken Nov. 21, 1900.

Name...George Parker, alias "Butch" Cassidy, alias George Cassidy, alias Ingerfield.
Nationality.................American
Occupation................Cowboy; rustler
Criminal Occupation......Bank robber and highwayman, cattle and horse thief
Age....36 yrs. (1901)......Height....5 feet 9 in
Weight...165 lbs..........Build.......Medium
Complexion...Light...Color of Hair..Flaxen
Eyes....Blue............Mustache, Sandy, if any
Remarks:—"Butch" Cassidy is known as a criminal principally in Wyoming, Utah, Idaho, Colorado and Nevada and has served time in Wyoming State penitentiary at Laramie for grand larceny, but was pardoned January 19th, 1896. Two cut scars back of head, small scar under left eye, small brown mole calf of leg.

HARRY LONGBAUGH.
Photograph taken Nov. 21, 1900.

Name........Harry Longbaugh, alias "Kid" Longbaugh, alias Harry Alonzo, alias Frank Jones, alias Frank Boyd, alias the "Sundance Kid"
Nationality.......Swedish-American. Occupation............Cowboy; rustler
Criminal Occupation ....Highwayman, bank burglar, cattle and horse thief
Age.........35 years...........Height.............5 feet 10 in
Weight......165 to 175 lbs............Build................Good
Eyes......Blue or gray............Complexion...........Medium
Mustache or Beard...........(if any), natural color brown, reddish tinge
Features............Grecian type.......Nose...........Rather long
Color of Hair............Natural color brown, may be dyed ; combs it pompadour.
IS BOW-LEGGED AND HIS FEET FAR APART.
Remarks:—Harry Longbaugh served 18 months in jail at Sundance, Cook Co., Wyoming, when a boy, for horse stealing. In December, 1892, Harry Longbaugh, Bill Madden and Henry Bass "held up" a Great Northern train at Malta, Montana. Bass and Madden were tried for this crime, convicted and sentenced to 10 and 14 years respectively ; Longbaugh escaped and since has been a fugitive. June 28, 1897, under the name of Frank Jones, Longbaugh participated with Harvey Logan, alias Curry, Tom Day and Walter Putney, in the Belle Fourche, South Dakota, bank robbery. All were arrested, but Longbaugh and Harvey Logan escaped from jail at Deadwood, October 31, the same year. Longbaugh has not since been arrested.

We also publish below a photograph, history and description of CAMILLA HANKS, alias O. C. HANKS, alias CHARLEY JONES, alias DEAF CHARLEY, who may be found in the company of either PARKER, alias CASSIDY or LONGBAUGH, alias ALONZO, and for whom a proportionate amount of a $5,000.00 Reward is offered by the GREAT NORTHERN EXPRESS COMPANY upon arrest and conviction for participation in the Great Northern (Railway) Express robbery near Wagner, Mont., July 3rd, 1901.

CAMILLA HANKS.
Photograph taken 1901.

Name...O. C. Hanks, alias Camilla Hanks, alias Charley Jones, alias Deaf Charley
Nationality...........American.......Occupation....................Cowboy
Criminal Occupation........Train robber ; an ex-convict
Age.........38 years (1901)........Height............5 feet 10 in
Weight......156 lbs................Build...................Good
Complexion......Sandy..............Color of Hair...........Auburn
Eyes......Blue................Mustache or Beard......(if any), natural color sandy
Remarks:—Scar from burn, size 25c piece, on right forearm. Small scar right leg, above ankle. Mole near right nipple. Leans his head slightly to the left. Somewhat deaf. Raised at Yorktown, Texas, fugitive from there charged with rape ; also wanted in New Mexico on charge of murder. Arrested in Teton County, Montana, 1892, and sentenced to 10 years in the penitentiary at Deer Lodge, Montana, for holding up Northern Pacific train near Big Timber, Montana. Released April 30th, 1901.

HARVEY LOGAN, alias "KID" CURRY, referred to in our first circular issued from Denver on May 15, 1901, is now under arrest at Knoxville, Tenn., charged with shooting two police officers who were attempting his arrest.

BEN KILPATRICK, alias JOHN ARNOLD, alias "THE TALL TEXAN" of Concho County, Texas, another member of the Harvey Logan band of outlaws, was arrested at St. Louis, Mo., on November 5th, 1901, tried, convicted and sentenced to 15 years imprisonment for participation in the robbery of the GREAT NORTHERN EXPRESS COMPANY, near Wagner, Mont.

WILLIAM CARVER, alias "BILL" CARVER, of Sonora, Sutton County, Texas, another member of this band, was killed at Sonora, Texas, by Sheriff E. S. Briant, while resisting arrest on charge of murder.

IN CASE OF AN ARREST immediately notify PINKERTON'S NATIONAL DETECTIVE AGENCY at the nearest of the above listed offices.

Or
JOHN C. FRASER, Resident Sup't., DENVER, COLO.

Pinkerton's National Detective Agency,
Opera House Block, Denver, Colo.

The Pinkerton's "Wanted" poster
for the Wild Bunch gang

rious, however, for the many people he needlessly shot dead. Horn became a paid killer after he stopped working for the Pinkertons. He was hanged in 1901 for the death of a young boy he accidentally shot.

Adams Express was not the only company to take an important role in fighting train robbery. In 1875, the Southern Express announced their messengers would defend themselves and their cars if they were attacked.

Other express companies followed their example. They all agreed that messengers who killed outlaws would be paid a reward.

Wells-Fargo messenger Aaron Ross took company policy seriously. On January 23, 1883, outlaws attacked Ross in his express car. He refused to open the door for them. They sprayed the car with bullets, rammed it with the locomotive, and tried to set it on fire. After everything failed, they gave up and rode away in disgust.

When Ross returned to his home in San Francisco, California, Wells-Fargo gave him a hero's welcome. They wanted a message sent to train robbers everywhere: it would take more than bullets to break a Wells-Fargo messenger.

But Wells-Fargo did not just rely on the bravery of its messengers. West of the Rockies, the company formed its own detective force. It was led by James B. Hume, a proud and loyal employee.

**Tom Horn was hanged after this
jury found him guilty.**

Hume called his detectives "special officers." They never used disguises. Instead, Hume and his force relied on informers, or "snitches," to give them information about the train robbers they hunted.

The capture rate for train robbers was surprisingly high. Over eighty percent of all robbers were either captured or killed. But the outlaws were not discouraged by their slim chance of success. Train robbery was easy. The number of robberies continued to grow, and so did the costs of catching the outlaws.

By the mid-1890s, express companies often spent ten times more money chasing train robbers than what was lost in the robberies. The Pinkertons, famous for never giving up on a case, proudly announced they would spend $20,000 to catch a thief who stole only $2,000.

Everyone agreed that the cost of catching train robbers was too high. There had to be a better solution to the problem.

William Pinkerton believed that the newspapers made things worse. He accused them of "filling the youthful mind with . . . a desire for notoriety and adventure."

It was true that some newspapers wrote stories that made the robberies seem more exciting than they really were. In one case, a rather ordinary ranch hand who held up two trains in Wisconsin in 1889 was

This drawing is entitled
"Still Another Big
Railroad Robbery,"
a comment on how common
the crime had become.

$18,000.00
REWARD

Union Pacific Railroad and Pacific Express Companies jointly, will pay $2,000.00 per head, dead or alive, for the six robbers who held up Union Pacific mail and express train ten miles west of Rock Creek Station, Albany County, Wyoming, on the morning of June 2nd, 1899.

The United States Government has also offered a reward of $1,000.00 per head, making in all $3,000.00 for each of these robbers.

Three of the gang described below, are now being pursued in northern Wyoming; the other three are not yet located, but doubtless soon will be.

DESCRIPTION: One man about 32 years of age; height, five feet, nine inches; weight 185 pounds; complexion and hair, light; eyes, light blue; peculiar nose, flattened at bridge and heavy at point; round, full, red face; bald forehead; walks slightly stooping; when last seen wore No. 8 cow-boy boots.

Two men, look like brothers, complexion, hair and eyes, very dark; larger one, age about 30; height, five feet, five inches; weight, 145 pounds; may have slight growth of whiskers; smaller one, age about 28; height, five feet, seven inches; weight 135 pounds; sometimes wears moustache.

Any information concerning these bandits should be promptly forwarded to Union Pacific Railroad Company and to the United States Marshal of Wyoming, at Cheyenne.

UNION PACIFIC RAILROAD COMPANY.
PACIFIC EXPRESS COMPANY.

Omaha, Nebraska, June 10th, 1899.

It could cost thousands of dollars to catch train robbers— if they could be caught!

written up as "Black Bart of Wisconsin." In another, "the most daring holdup thus far" turned out to be no different from earlier robberies.

But officials did not pay attention to Pinkerton's demands for better reporting. Instead, they decided to make the trains stronger.

Express companies had started rebuilding their cars as early as 1878. Unfortunately, after 1890, dynamite was used in one of every four robberies. This explosive could easily blow holes in the side of the strongest car.

To protect the valuables, dynamite-proof safes were built. At the same time, Wells-Fargo and other express companies began to experiment with time-lock, variable-combination-lock, and double-lock safes. They hoped to convince robbers that express messengers could not open a safe on demand.

With train robbery so much in the newspaper headlines, amateur inventors became interested in solving the problem. Many suggested turning express cars into "tanks," topped with searchlights and revolving Gatling guns (early machine guns). Some inventors suggested putting electrically charged metal strips on the floor of the express car to electrocute the outlaws. Others favored filling the express car with burning hot steam, spraying the outlaws with boiling water, or covering them with boiling oil.

People often came up with opposite ways of solving the problem. One person urged the railroads to give passengers hand grenades to toss out the windows at the bandits. Another wanted to ban all explosives, so robbers could not get the dynamite they needed.

Most suggestions were well meant, but not practical. The railroads did try a few of the ideas with some success.

One plan included sending a code signal for help (a series of whistle blasts) from a train in trouble to another train or a nearby station.

A second plan involved filling the safe with wrapped packages of blank paper. The actual money was stored elsewhere. An express company used this scheme on the Dalton gang during a holdup on the Santa Fe line in 1891. The gang was miles away before they realized they had been tricked.

A few outlaws were trapped by a decoy train. When a railroad happened to learn of a planned robbery, they loaded the express car with a posse instead of money.

Some railway officials wanted to change United States law instead of trying to outsmart the criminals. Twenty-five years after the first holdup in Seymour, there was still no law that made train robbery a federal crime.

William Pinkerton declared, "If it becomes a crime against the United States government to hold up a train, it is almost certain that this class of work will soon come to an end."

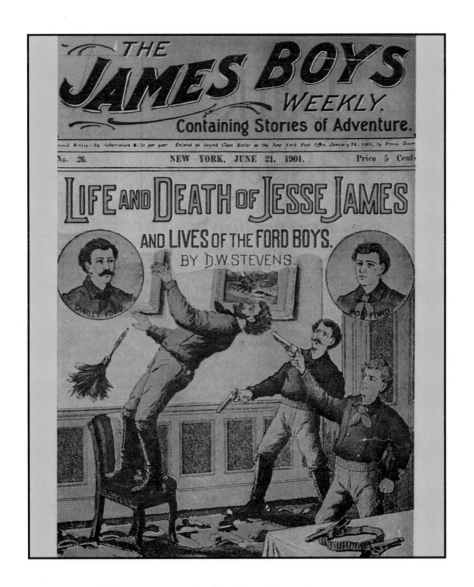

Dime novels helped make some
bandits famous. Here, Jesse James's
death is dramatized for readers.

In 1893, both the United States Congress and the Senate tried to pass bills that would make train robbery a federal offense. But the details of the law were criticized and argued. Finally, the vote was put off indefinitely.

Despite good intentions, the problem of train robbery continued in the United States.

CHAPTER FOUR

AN END IN SIGHT

Between 1890 and 1899, the number of train robberies reached its peak in the United States. In May of 1893, robbers struck three different railroads on the same night. In January 1894, holdups in Missouri occurred almost once a week.

During this time, good-natured outlaw Bill Doolin, who had ridden with the Daltons until their deaths, formed his own gang. He left a trail of robberies in Kansas and Oklahoma for two years before he was shot and killed.

The Wild Bunch was active in Wyoming. In Oklahoma, "Dynamite Dick" Clifton and ex-lawyer Al Jennings teamed up. The Clifton-Jennings gang, an unlucky band, held up half a dozen trains before they were caught.

Then, almost overnight, several changes took place to discourage train robbery. Suddenly, the holdups dropped to less than ten per year.

In 1898, E. H. Harriman took over the Union Pacific Railroad. Harriman put together armed posses that operated out of "horse cars"—special baggage cars pulled by fast trains. The cars carried the posses to the scene of the robbery in less than an hour. With armed lawmen just one step behind them, the bandits lost the time they needed to get away.

Seeing Harriman's success, other law enforcement agencies copied the Union Pacific's methods.

More Changes

By 1900, even small prairie towns were being connected by telegraph lines. Detective and law enforcement agencies were popping up all across the West. Outlaws had to search harder to find the isolated areas they needed to hold up the trains.

Shipments of gold and silver from the West were tapering off. Passengers began carrying traveler's checks instead of cash. A robber had less chance of finding the treasure he had easily taken in the past.

Finally, in 1902, Congress passed the federal Train Robbery Act. It was now a federal crime to board a

This posse is ready to catch the thieves who robbed a Union Pacific train in Tipton, Wyoming. Once the practice of organizing posses had begun, train robbers had more difficulty evading capture.

train with the intent to rob it. Outlaws were faced with tougher penalties when they were caught.

On January 1, 1913, Congress authorized the parcel post system. Express companies quickly went out of business because money and valuables were shipped by mail. Although the mail was still carried by train, now robbers had to either sort through the mail or steal huge bags of letters to find the loot.

The years that favored train robbers had come and gone. In 1907, William Pinkerton declared the train robber an "almost extinct outlaw." Although robbery was riskier than ever before, there were still men willing to take the risks.

Bill Carlisle was such a man. He seemed to enjoy danger. While riding the Union Pacific in Wyoming on February 4, 1916, an idea popped into his head: "Why not stick up a train!"

He had made no plans and didn't know how he would get away. Nevertheless, Carlisle tied a white handkerchief over his face and pulled off the robbery. He carried a toy pistol while he gathered up the money.

Carlisle was a thief, but he had his principles. He earned the name "Gentleman Bandit" because he refused to steal from women or soldiers. When two men were mistakenly imprisoned for one of Carlisle's robberies, he sent a letter to the *Denver Post:*

To convince the officers that they have the wrong men in jail, I will hold up a train somewhere west of Laramie, Wyoming. (signed) The White Masked Bandit.

Carlisle kept his promise and robbed another train on April 21, 1916. He was finally captured in December 1919 in a wilderness cabin in Wyoming. He was imprisoned and became a model prisoner. Carlisle was paroled in 1936. He spent the rest of his life writing and speaking against crime and juvenile delinquency.

Like Carlisle, train robber Roy Gardner ignored danger. He began robbing the mail in Southern California on April 27, 1920, and successfully robbed mail cars on several midwestern railroads.

Known as the "King of the Escape Artists," Gardner tricked his guards and escaped three times. He got away twice on his way to prison. His third escape was on September 5, 1921, from McNeil Penitentiary, an island prison surrounded by the icy waters of Puget Sound off Washington State.

Gardner never gave up trying to escape, but despite his daring, he was always caught. He was one of the first men to be sent to the United States government's new "escape-proof" prison on Alcatraz Island in San Francisco Bay.

The brutal D'Autremont brothers—Roy, Ray and

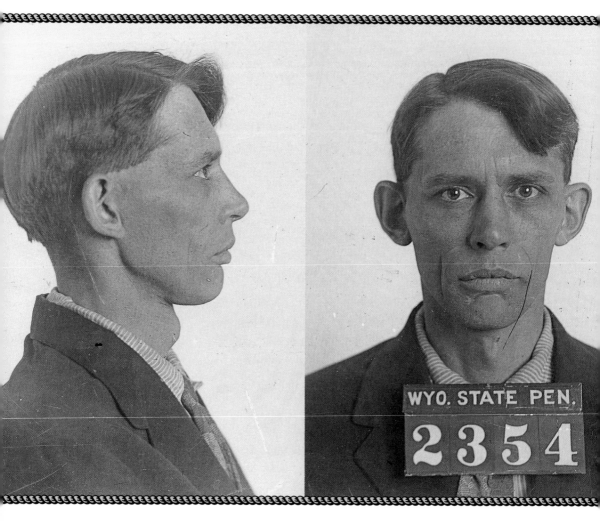

**Bill Carlisle, here in his
prison photo, reformed while in
Wyoming State Penitentiary.**

Hugh—were long remembered for their single train robbery on October 11, 1923.

The brothers stopped a Southern Pacific passenger train in a tunnel in Southern Oregon. They dynamited the mail car, killing the clerk and filling the car with smoke. Unable to get to the money through the smoke, the brothers shot down three of the crew in cold blood. They then escaped empty-handed.

The search for the D'Autremont brothers was called the "greatest manhunt ever." It took four years and a worldwide effort before all three brothers were caught. For the first time in history, the most modern methods were used to track the outlaws. An airplane helped in the search. Criminologist Edward Oscar Heinrich, the "Edison of crime detection," was called in to help. His work led to the capture of the brothers.

The Last Episode

The last train robbery in the United States is remembered because it ended a notorious period of history. The robbery itself was not successful. The train robbers were forgettable men.

The incident took place in late 1937 on the Southern Pacific line near El Paso, Texas. Shortly after midnight, two young men from the Midwest decided to rob the passengers.

W. L. Smith, a former switchman for the railroad, was one of the passengers. He watched as the young bandits pulled guns and began collecting the passengers' cash. Smith was a large, brave man. As one of the robbers walked down the aisle, Smith grabbed for the man's gun.

While Smith wrestled with one bandit, another passenger tripped the other one. When the young gunman fell, the passenger fell on him.

Suddenly, the rest of the men in the car joined in the attack. The two young robbers were jumped on, beaten, and kicked. Finally, they were hauled off unconscious to jail. The age of train robbery was over.

The railroads still watch carefully to make sure they are safe from modern-day train robbers. They hope that would-be robbers take the advice of outlaw Emmett Dalton, who wrote:

> The biggest fool on earth is the one who thinks he can beat the law, that crime can be made to pay.

GLOSSARY

Barricade—something that blocks the way.

Blind baggage—a platform at the front of a window-less express car where train robbers could board a train unseen by the express messenger, train crew, or passengers.

Criminologist—a person who studies crime and criminals.

Crossties—the heavy wooden beams that lie cross-wise to the metal rails of a railroad track.

Decoy—a person or thing used to trap something else.

Depot—a railroad station.

Express car—a railroad car that carried the gold,

valuables, and important papers shipped by an express company.

Express company—a company responsible for moving gold, valuables, and important papers quickly and safely from one point to another.

Horse cars—special railroad cars that carried posses and their horses to the scene of a train robbery.

Isolated—set apart from other people or places.

Juvenile delinquency—behavior by young people that is against the law.

Long rider—an outlaw who traveled long distances from the scene of the crime before he stopped to rest.

Loot—1. money or items of value.
2. to steal.

Notorious—known for bad deeds.

Operative—a detective.

Penalty—a punishment set by law.

Posse—a band of armed men, led by a law officer, used to catch outlaws or keep peace.

Relay—a fresh supply of animals kept to take the place of others when they tire.

Running board—a narrow walkway along the lower edge of the side of a railroad car.

Ruthless—cruel, without pity.

Scald—to burn with hot water or steam.

Switch—a section of movable track used to transfer trains from one railroad to another.

Tender—a railroad car that carried coal and water for the steam engine.

Time-lock safe—a safe that cannot be opened until a period of time has passed.

Torpedo signal—a tiny, harmless explosive, clamped to a railroad track, that made a loud noise when a train ran over it.

NOTES

Page 17 "When you see the reporters, tell 'em you were talking to Jesse James!"

Richard Patterson, *Train Robbery: The Birth, Flowering and Decline of A Notorious Western Enterprise*. Boulder, CO: Johnson Publishing, 1981.

Page 36 "an almost unshakable bloodhound"

Richard Patterson, *Train Robbery: The Birth, Flowering*, etc.

Page 40 "filling the youthful mind with . . . a desire for notoriety and adventure."

William Pinkerton, *Train Robberies, Train Robbers and Holdup Men*. New York: Arno Press, 1974.

Page 44 "If it becomes a crime against the United States government to hold up a train," etc. . . . .

William Pinkerton, *Train Robberies, Train Robbers and Holdup Men.*

Page 50 "almost extinct outlaw"

William Pinkerton, *Train Robberies, Train Robbers and Holdup Men.*

Pages 50–51 "Why not stick up a train?" and "To convince the officers that they have the wrong men in jail . . ."

William Carlisle, *Bill Carlisle, Lone Bandit, An Autobiography.* Pasadena, CA: Trail's End Publishing, 1946.

Page 54 "The biggest fool on earth is the one who thinks he can beat the law, that crime can be made to pay."

James D. Horan & Paul Sann, *Pictorial History of the Wild West.* New York: Crown Publishers, 1954.

FOR FURTHER READING

Cook, Fred J. *The Pinkertons*. New York: Doubleday, 1974.

Ernst, John. *Jesse James*. Englewood Cliffs, NJ: Prentice Hall, 1976.

Johnson, Dorothy M. *Western Badmen*. New York: Dodd, Mead, 1976.

Orrimont, Arthur. *Allan Pinkerton: Master Detective*. New York: J. Messner, 1965.

INDEX

ABOUT THE AUTHOR

Diane Yancey grew up in Grass Valley, California, across the street from the once-famous Empire Gold Mine. Long ago, train robbers Butch Cassidy and the Sundance Kid might have stolen gold being transported east from the Empire Mine.

While *Desperadoes and Dynamite* is her first published work, Mrs. Yancey has been writing for her own entertainment since she was thirteen years old. She now pursues a writing career in the Pacific Northwest, where she lives with her husband, two daughters, and two cats.